B A T S

Shadows in the Night

by Diane Ackerman

PHOTOGRAPHS BY
MERLIN TUTTLE

Crown Publishers, Inc., New York

Previous page: Thousands of Mexican free-tailed bats
emerge from Bracken Cave, Texas.

Parts of this book first appeared in a different version in *The Moon
by Whale Light* by Diane Ackerman, published by Random House,
Inc. Copyright © 1991 by Diane Ackerman.

Published by Crown Publishers, Inc., a Random House company,
201 East 50th Street, New York, New York 10022.

CROWN is a trademark of Crown Publishers, Inc.
Printed in Hong Kong
http://www.randomhouse.com/

Library of Congress Cataloging-in-Publication Data
Ackerman, Diane.
Bats: Shadows in the night / by Diane Ackerman ; photographs by
Merlin Tuttle.
        p.   cm.
Summary: The author gets to see bats close up as she accompanies
bat expert and founder of Bat Conservation International Merlin
Tuttle on a trip to study these often misunderstood mammals.
1. Bats—Juvenile literature. [1. Bats.] I. Tuttle, Merlin D., ill. II.
Title.
QL737.C5A18   1997
599.4—dc20   96-6047

ISBN 0-517-70919-8 (trade) — 0-517-70920-1 (lib. bdg.)
10 9 8 7 6 5 4 3 2 1
First Edition

One hot, humid summer night, I lie down on the grass in my backyard, under a sky speckled with stars, and wait for bats to appear. Three little brown bats live in the woods nearby, and though I don't see them every evening, I feel lucky when I do. A bright flashing satellite cruises across the sky, appearing out of darkness to dazzle all with its speed and clarity, before it sinks again into the upside-down well of the heavens. There are more constellations on view than I have ever seen before, so many that they seem to be nesting inside each other. The Milky Way is a long backbone of light, just as the Bushmen of the Kalahari call it. A frog croaks a deep, throaty *I am,* and others sound like creaking doors and some like girls throwing smoochy kisses. There is nothing to do now but wait. It is always like this for naturalists, and for poets—the long hours of waiting. All for that one electric, pulse-revving moment when the universe suddenly declares itself. A view of life so astonishing as to make all of life newly astonishing. A bat would do niccly.

Little brown bat (*Myotis lucifugus*).

3

Suddenly, two little brown bats appear at the end of the yard and flutter toward the house, flying the length of the eaves before swooping around a tree and heading into the woods. Hungry, they're dining on the evening air's throng of insects. Wonderful, bats! But not nearly enough of them. I've always been fascinated by bats, flying mammals that can grow to colossal size (some have wingspans of six feet!). Misunderstood night creatures, they are winged mysteries, the stuff of myth and legend. I regard bats as wonderful neighbors, and I'd love to see more of them, maybe even millions more.

Above and right: Little brown bats in flight.

4

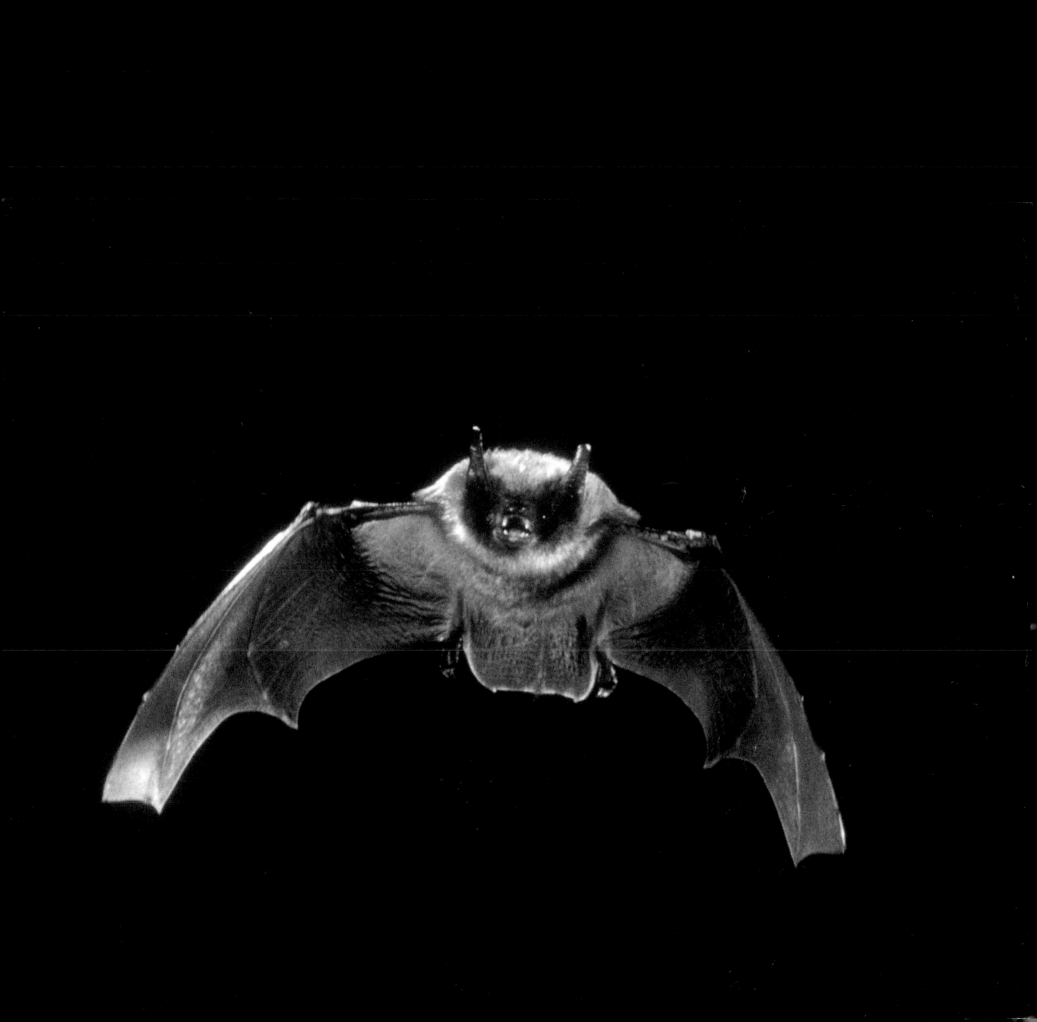

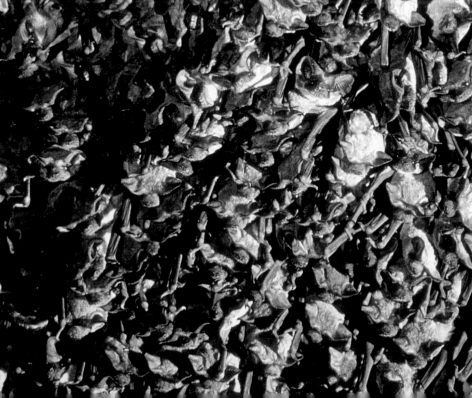

A few weeks later, I travel to Texas, rent a car, and drive to a famous cave near San Antonio. There I take a seat in a natural amphitheater of limestone boulders, at the bottom of which is the wide, dark mouth of Bracken Cave. Nothing stirs yet in its depths. But I have been promised one of the wonders of our age. Deep inside the cavern, 20 million Mexican free-tailed bats are hanging by their toes. They are the largest concentration of warm-blooded animals in the world. At dusk, all 20 million of them will fly out to feed, in a living volcano scientists call an "emergence." They will flood the sky with their leathery wings and ultrasonic cries, and people in San Antonio, without realizing it, will rarely be more than seventy feet from a feeding bat.

"I've sometimes sat here for three hours and still seen them pouring out," the man next to me says, radiant with anticipation. If anyone should know their habits, it is my friend Merlin D. Tuttle, a leading authority on bats, founder and director of Bat Conservation International (BCI), and an explorer. On the ground beside us lie some of the tools of his trade: an infrared nightscope that allows one to see in the dark; a miner's headlamp powered by a large heavy battery that he carries in a

Bracken Cave (above), its walls covered with millions of densely clustered Mexican free-tailed bats (below).

khaki ammunition belt around his waist; a "mini bat-detector," an electronic device that picks up the echolocating calls of many species of bats, which are inaudible to human ears. Noticeably absent are gloves, sticks, or other protective or defensive things.

"Bats are among the gentlest of animals," he says. "They're really shy and winsome creatures who have just had bad press. When you see bats as they really are, they're just as inquisitive, comical, and cute as other animals. The only bats people tend to see are ones that are sick or dying. They find them lying on the ground someplace; naturally, the bat opens its mouth wide, bares its teeth, trying to scare them away, and that's the image they get. But we ourselves wouldn't come across too well if people saw us only when we were dying or sick."

Before I can say anything, his eyes dart to the cave mouth, and a smile drifts over his face along with the fading rays of sunlight. I follow his gaze. Hundreds of small bats have appeared suddenly, darting and climbing, swirling and looping. Then they spiral up and scroll off to the east. It's a small, odd spectacle.

"Just wait," Merlin says, reading my mind.

Emergence at Bracken Cave.

Small dark clouds begin to swell, spinning like an open funnel as the bats orbit until they're high enough to depart. Like airplanes in a mountain valley, they must circle to climb, so they whisk around one another, wing to wing, in tight echelons. As they revolve, they pick up speed. Over open country, free-tailed bats can cruise at 35 mph. Shadows march through the trees as the whirlpooling bats set off on a night's cross-country journey to forage for food. A natural pesticide, they eat 200 tons of insects every night.

As wave upon wave of bats pours out of the cave, their collective wings begin to sound like drizzle on autumn leaves. Swirling fast in the living Mixmaster, newly risen bats start in close then veer out almost to the rim of the bowl, climbing until they're high enough to clear the ridge. Already the long black column of bats looks like a tornado spinning far across the Texas sky. The night is silent, except for the serene beating of their wings.

Such a gush of bats flows upward that two columns form, each thick and beating, making long pulsing ribbons, climbing high to ride rapid air currents to distant feeding sites. Some groups twist into a bow shape, others into a tuning fork, then a claw, a wrench, a waving hand. Buffeted by uneven currents, they make the air visible, as it rarely is. In the rosy dusk, their wings beat so fast that it looks as if a strobe light is playing over them.

"Follow that albino one!" Merlin says suddenly, pointing to the cave entrance, where a white ball has just appeared among what looks like a swarm of flying black peppercorns. One, two, three circuits of the bowl. It drifts far out to the rim toward us, its mouth open, then it floats over the ridge and joins one of the columns.

Gesturing with one hand as if to press down a stack of invisible myths, he says, "Their mouths are open when they fly because they need them that way to echolocate. They're not snarling or mean; they're just trying not to bump into anything. That's how their sonar works. Look, I'll show you."

Mexican free-tailed bat (*Tadarida brasiliensis mexicana*).

Two columns of bats spread out across the Texas sky

Bat Essentials

Name of order: Chiroptera, meaning "hand wing."

Almost 1,000 species, divided into two groups:

Megachiroptera ("big" bats): About 200 species, including flying foxes, living in the world's warm tropical regions.

Microchiroptera ("small" bats): About 800 species, living on every continent except Antarctica.

Biggest bats: Flying foxes, which weigh up to four pounds, with wingspans up to six feet.

Smallest bat: Bumblebee bat (Thailand), which weighs less than two grams.

Lifespan: An average of 15 years; some bats may live as long as 34 years.

Food: Insects, fruit, nectar, fish, frogs, and other small animals, depending on species.

With that, he leads me down into the center of the bowl, toward the cave, right into the thick of the swarming, fluttering bats, which fly around our shoulders, over our heads, beside my chin. Too amazed to flinch, I can feel them graze my head with their flutters without actually touching me with their wings. The breeze they make blows my long hair back. We are standing in the middle of 20 million wild bats. Merlin swings both arms above his head, then does it again. On the third time, he grabs a bat right out of the air.

Climbing back up to our original spot, I sit down on a boulder beside him to see what he's captured. Its wings held closed by his grip, its small furry brown head sticking out, a little bat looks up at us, frightened and fragile. It uses its chin as a pry bar, trying to escape, but makes no attempt to bite.

"See how ferocious he is?" Merlin says.

The face is gnomelike, the body covered with a thick, fluffy brown fur. What must it make of us—large, powerful animals with big eyes and big teeth? It opens its mouth to echolocate but doesn't snap or nip, and, in any case, its teeth are very small. Merlin loosens his grip a little. Still holding the wings closed with one hand, he strokes its back with the other, and the little bat quiets down. I know better than to pick up a bat I might see lying on the ground, or any wild animal acting abnormally, for that matter. But a veteran bat handler snatching a healthy bat out of the air is different.

"Want to touch?" he asks.

Mexican free-tailed bats.

I run a finger over the tiny back, feel the slender bones and the soft fur. Then we open out the wings and I stroke their dark, thin, rubbery membrane, trace the elongated fingers that hold up the wings, and look at the tail from which the free-tailed bat gets its name. The scientific name for all bats is Chiroptera, "hand wing," and even on a small version like this one the hand wings are clear.

"Isn't he a winsome little fellow?" Merlin asks. "Here, you can let him go." When he places the bat on my open palm, I feel a swift scuttle as it creeps wing over wing to my fingertips, then launches itself into the air to rejoin its colony, which now has filled the entire sky with black magic.

Merlin Tuttle at Bracken Cave.

Safety

Like other wild animals, bats can transmit disease, including rabies. Left alone, bats present very little danger to humans, but because sick animals are the easiest to find, you should *never* handle a wild bat—or any other wild animal. Never attempt to catch a bat or to keep one in captivity. Only experienced animal rehabilitators, educators, or researchers should handle wild animals.

arly the next day, Merlin and I begin a journey in a light plane, four hundred miles southwest from Austin into the Big Bend National Park area, where we hope to net and photograph several species of bats. When most people think of a bat, they picture the simple little brown bat. But what a carnival of bats inhabits the world! There is the epauletted fruit bat, which has handsome tufts of fur on its shoulders and wraps its

Above: Hammer-headed fruit bat (*Hypsignathus monstrosus*).
Left: Gambian epauletted fruit bat (*Epomophorus gambianus*).

wings around itself like a blanket when it rests; the African hammer-headed fruit bat, which has a long, mitered-off face, like a horse that has been punched in the nose; the spectacled flying fox, which has a sharp foxlike face, black eyes ringed with white fur, and keen vision; the Mexican funnel-eared bat, which looks like a golden Pekingese dog; the sword-nosed bat, whose ears and nose leaf are almost as long as its body;

Clockwise from upper right: Spectacled flying fox (*Pteropus conspicillatus*), sword-nosed bat (*Lonchorhina aurita*), Mexican funnel-eared bat (*Natalus stramineus*).

the African yellow-winged bat, with big eyes, long silky fur, and brilliant yellow wings; the greater horseshoe bat, which has horseshoe-shaped leaves surrounding its nostrils that look like a nebula; the Egyptian fruit bat, with a small squirrel-like face, which wraps one wing protectively around its sweetheart when it's ready to mate, and whose young are born with a human-looking, scrunched-up face; the crested free-tailed bat, which puffs up its head crest during courtship; the long-eared bat, with pleated ears it can fold up and tuck under its wings; the

Above: African yellow-winged bat (*Lavia frons*).
Right: Greater horseshoe bat (*Rhinolophus ferrumequinum*).

common vampire, with a cleft chin and a pitted nose full of heat-sensing devices; the Mexican free-tailed bat, whose face is so wrinkled it looks like a wise old extraterrestrial. A complete gallery of bats would take ages to compile, and Merlin has been doing just that—patiently photographing a lifetime of bat study.

Clockwise from upper left: Egyptian fruit bat (*Rousettus aegyptiacus*), long-eared bat (*Plecotus auritus*), crested free-tailed bat (*Chaerephon chapini*), common vampire bat (*Desmodus rotundus*).

Big Bend National Park, Texas.

At the airport, we meet Don Grantges and his twelve-year-old son, Bert. Don is our pilot, and Bert is a junior naturalist and bat enthusiast himself who keeps six bats at their home in Fort Worth, Texas. He and his family all have had the appropriate vaccinations so they can be involved with Merlin's research.

Soon we are up and aloft, floating over the shiny black office building in which Merlin's Bat Conservation International is housed. Then the city gives way to the loopy fingerprints of the desert, the swirling patterns of sand and vegetation. In the distance lies the sinewy Rio Grande. Don flies toward the wilderness. There are no navigation beacons where we are going, and the desert pours by hypnotically below. Don has flown this route before and intuits his way among the mountain peaks and over the peppery sands to the park, where he swivels the plane around a wingtip, dipping, rolling out, and dipping again. Our eyes crawl over the ground, eating up the terrain, searching for pools of water shallow enough to wade into, close to potential roosting sites like rock cliffs. The plane's shadow over the ground looks like a black bat flying below us. Big Bend is bat country—lots of nooks and crevices for bats to roost in; lots of food for bats to eat.

An epauletted fruit bat in flight, carrying its pup.

Mexican free-tailed bat with pup.

At last, we land on a small crooked runway, beside which Carol Grantges waits to drive us to the nearby lodge, where we quickly unpack. Missing the evening's bats would be unthinkable. So, grabbing slabs of cheese and a handful of crackers, we pack the truck with Merlin's batting equipment and a cooler of drinks and drive down to a boggy site that, from the air, looked particularly promising.

Carol remarks that on one trip to Big Bend they caught 600 bats. "We caught fourteen different species," she adds. "There are only forty-five species of bats in North America. So that's pretty good going."

Baby Bats

Most species of bats give birth once a year and have only one baby, called a pup. The pups are born in the spring and feed on their mother's milk for about six weeks before they are weaned. In most species, pups make their first flight at about three weeks old.

A few species of bats carry their pups with them when they fly in search of food. Most leave them behind in huge clusters. When she returns, the mother bat identifies her pup by its special call and scent.

Just before dusk, we reach the site we're after: an oasis, where a small spring has fed a wealth of trees and bushes, tall drooping willows, cattails, a smear of algae, and many insects. Bats should find it a delectable place both to drink and dine.

Capturing bats for study isn't easy, since their sonar spins an intricate invisible web across the sky and, anyway, they tend to live in communal roosts high up along cliffs or, in South America, in the canopies of the rain forest, where few people have ventured, even now. A mist net is the solution. Like a long hairnet, a mist net stretches across the pond, with movable gussets so it can be opened as much as six feet wide. Echolocation sometimes doesn't work with netting as intangible as a mist net's, and there is a sense in which the net seems almost

magical. How do you capture the flying dragon? an ancient Japanese warrior might ask a wise man. Only with a net made of mist.

The sun has begun to drain behind the distant mountains, washing the sky, the people, and the small pond with an apricot glow. A light breeze drives small waves across the water. Thick cumulus clouds, and the black threads of the net, reflect in the water, and when Don wades in, concentric circles flow gently away from him. He leans back on the pole that will support the net, driving it into the mud. For a moment, it looks as if he is going to vault. Meanwhile, the water rises over his sneakers and short white socks. The sun glares off Merlin's gold-rimmed glasses as he presses his pole in deep. When they

pull the fine net taut, it becomes invisible. Walking its length, both men inspect it for holes, and they seem to be holding on to empty space, knotting empty space in their hands. Merlin's forearms are tanned to the Indian-red of the desert at twilight, and I have to squint hard to distinguish between him and the land.

Now, as night begins bluing and cooling down the desert, a few tiny pipistrelle bats flash above the trees to feed. With darkness falling fast, we lay out a blue tarpaulin with a Day-Glo orange sleeping bag spread over it, put on our miner's head-lamps, and stroll around the pond with the mini bat-detector. When Merlin turns the machine on, I flinch, and he laughs. The whirring, buzzing, creaking sounds that it spits out are made by insects. Turn it off and all is silence. How thrilling to discover the night packed with sounds one isn't normally aware of. Every few yards, pinprick eyes glitter at our feet, and Bert casts the light of his headlamp onto them, chasing spiders as they scramble in the dirt. Then the chattery racket on the bat-detector tells us that a cloud of pipistrelles is drifting over our heads to feed.

Western pipistrelle bat (*Pipistrellus hesperus*).

Echolocation

Most bat species are nocturnal, which means that they are active during the night. They "see" the insects they eat, as well as other objects, by using a system called "echolocation." A flying bat sends out a stream of clicks. By listening for the echoes, the bat can tell where another object is, how big it is, and how fast it is moving.

Most bats make these echolocation clicks with their mouths, although some use their noses. All Microchiroptera echolocate. Most Megachiroptera do not, relying instead on their eyesight and sense of smell to find food.

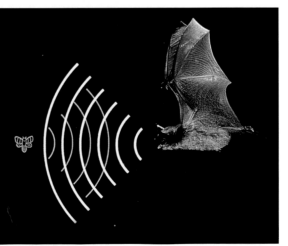

The large ears of many bat species, such as this slit-faced bat (*Nycteris hispida*), aid echolocation.

It's not hard to understand echolocation if you picture bats calling or whistling to their prey with a stream of high-frequency clicks. They don't click in a steady stream, but at irregular intervals ten to two hundred times a second. Bats listen for the sounds to return to them, and if the echoes start coming faster or louder, the bat knows the insect it's stalking has flown nearer. Judging the time between the echoes, a bat can tell how fast its prey is moving and in which direction. Some bats are even sensitive enough to hear a beetle walking on sand. Some can detect the movement of a moth flexing its wings as it sits on a leaf. As the bat closes in, it may click faster to pinpoint its prey. And there's a difference between the steady, solid echoes bouncing off a brick wall and the light, fluid echo of a swaying flower. By shouting at the world and listening to the echoes, bats can compose a picture of their landscape and the objects in it that includes texture, motion, distance, size, and probably other features, too. They shout very loudly; we just don't hear them. This is an eerie thought when one stands in a seemingly silent grove filled with bats. They spend their whole lives yelling at the world and each other. They yell at their loved ones, they yell at their enemies, they yell at their dinner, they yell at the big, bustling world. Some yell fast, some slow, some loud, some soft. Certain long-eared bats don't need to yell, since they can hear their echoes perfectly well if they whisper.

Above. A Mexican free-tailed bat catches a moth in flight.
Right: Spotted bat (*Euderma maculatum*).

Many bats' faces look like submarines covered with radar equipment. Horseshoe bats, for example, have oddly shaped noses with which to send out echolocation sounds.

Pipistrelles fill the sky, but what we're looking for is a rare, spectacularly colored creature, the spotted bat, which has pink translucent ears almost as long as its body, angora-like fur, a white belly, and a jet-black back with three white spots. It is the Dalmatian of the bat world. Not many of them have been captured, and few good photographs of them exist. Merlin has been after them for years. But none come our way tonight. Discouraged after several hours, we pack up the mist net and head back home. The night isn't lost yet. Maybe there will be pallid bats roosting at the lodge.

Sure enough, when we return we find a barn full of them clumped together like a geographical survey map: brown hills and valleys, with tiny scrunched-up faces peering out and long ears. Under the house eaves, more pallids huddle snugly together. Ecstatic, Merlin prepares his photo equipment, even though it's already 3:00 A.M. Don, Bert, and I hold the flashes and light meter, and off we tramp again through the night, trying to keep all our wires untangled. In the barn, we stand right under the bat-encrusted rafters. Then Merlin makes a cavalcade of noises to get the bats to prick up their ears, and he shoots frame after frame of pallid bats roosting in the wild. The bright flashes startle them just enough to make them urinate on our hands and shoulders, and a few frightened bats fly for darkness elsewhere in the barn. Some hide their faces in their arms like shy children. But Merlin is after a shot in

which a number of bats have a good "expression," as he puts it. Peccaries (a kind of wild pig) have been using the barn for their socializing, and the floor is squooshy with droppings and old wood and discarded lengths of metal. Bats wing around our heads in the darkness. Those huddled on the rafters peer down at us with tiny troll-like faces and are remarkably long-suffering. When he's sure he has some good photographs, Merlin calls it a night. We drag back to the lodge, leaving the equipment arrayed like an electronic explosion on the living room floor, and fall into our beds. The last thing I remember before falling asleep is the pallid bats huddled under the eaves of the lodge. It is almost impossible to describe their gentleness and sweetly expressive faces. When I wake and look outside, they are gone.

I suppose that would gladden some people, but I love bats.

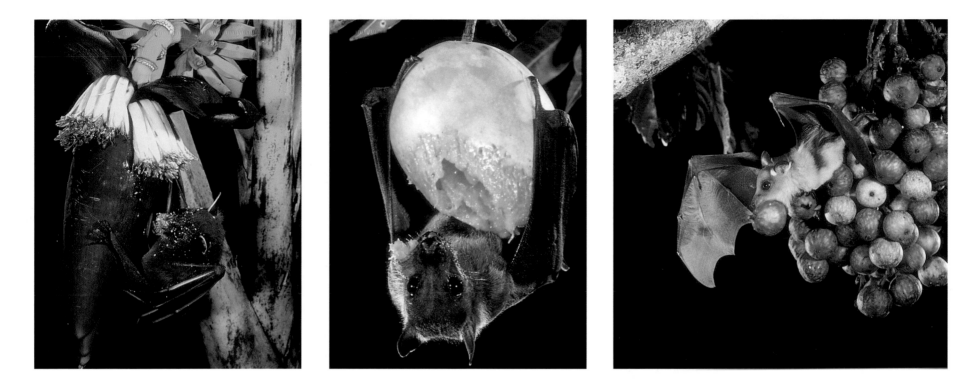

Fascinating and fun, bats are also good citizens of the planet. Here are just a few of the things we rely on bats for without realizing it: avocados, bananas, dates, figs, guavas, breadfruit, peaches, mangoes, carob, cloves, cashews, sisal for rope, kapok for life preservers and bandages, timber for furniture, chicle latex for chewing gum, balsa, and tequila. The disappearance of bats would sadly alter our world.

Some of the already extinct bats are the Jamaican long-tongued bat, a single specimen of which sits in a jar at the Institute of Jamaica; the Haitian long-tongued bat, whose habitats disappeared to developers; the tree-dwelling lesser falcate-winged bat of Cuba, which has been extinct for as long as 200 years; the Puerto Rican long-nosed bat, which had a distinctive long tail, and so was long at both ends; and the Cuban yellow bat, which had willowy legs and funnel-shaped ears.

Above from left: Pollen covers the face of a feeding short-nosed fruit bat (*Cynopterus sphinx*); Egyptian fruit bat; Gambian epauletted fruit bat carrying fruit in its jaws.

Feeding

Many species of bats eat fruit. They swallow, but cannot digest, the seeds. They pass the seeds in their droppings, enabling new trees to grow. Other species feed on the nectar and pollen of flowering plants. As these bats travel from flower to flower, they spread the pollen, helping the plants to reproduce. In the southwestern United States and Mexico, several species of cactus depend on bats to spread their pollen in this way.

Insect-eating bats are also helpful to the environment. They are a natural pesticide, controlling the insects that destroy crops and spread disease.

ager to find bats, we set off once more in the evening, following an old mining road that becomes a six-mile rodeo ride in the high-bucking pickup truck. When we arrive at the site, it feels good to get out at last and stretch our legs, unpack our gear, and hike up the rock-strewn creek bed, dry now in the diabolical heat. Here and there small ponds hold thousands of tadpoles, and slick gray rocks look like basking seals. Red dragonflies plane low over the deep black water, with giant hornets and other insects doing dogfights in the air.

Above: Peter's ghost-faced bat (*Mormoops megalophylla*).
Right: Merlin Tuttle and Bert Grantges examine a bat caught in the mist net.

At 8:10 P.M., a large billowy storm blows south of us, with swelling gray-blue clouds and the tinges of electric green I know to be the signature of hail. Sunlight cuts through the clouds, twisting like knife blades, and then makes corridors of light that seem almost walkable. When night falls, lightning continues to prowl around the south rim of the gorge. Coyotes yowl in the distance. Shooting stars begin to streak the sky with their white tears. Time for the miner's headlamps, the mini bat-detectors, and the vigil for the spotted bat.

A dark flutter at eye level disappears, and that fast its *ping-ping, ping-ping, ping-ping* disappears with it. We look down at the net, hidden in the dark and shadows. Merlin flashes his headlamp over the flimsy strings of mist, picks up his infrared nightscope, and looks more carefully. Nothing. But at the next net, one pole is bobbing. For bat catchers, a sure sign. Don and Bert leap to the net and begin disentangling the small bat, which is caught in the overlapping beams of their headlamps. Illumination is what passes between father and son. It is not a spotted but a ghost-faced bat, one of Bert's favorites, a little squinting face in a fluffy parka of fur. Then we catch a free-tailed bat, just like those I saw at Bracken Cave. Merlin shows us how the tail slides in and out like a sword concealed in an English walking cane. On its wings, red veins make a Christmas tree design.

"Can I hold him?" Bert asks, reaching out a finger as if for a pet parakeet to step onto. The bat hooks its feet around Bert's finger and hangs upside down, unalarmed. Then Bert swings it gently like a small brown hammock, and it rolls to one side and takes flight at the same moment. With the bat flown, it's time to return to our stations and await the next arrival. We lie on our backs in the still of the Texas night, with the occasional click of an elusive spotted bat overhead, the stars yodeling light, the coyotes howling, the meteors throwing their small bouquets, and peace everlasting.

Mexican free-tailed bat.

When we return to Austin the next day, I visit Merlin at his office at Bat Conservation International, where he has a library of books and articles about bats. Today he also has two bats hanging upside down in a mesh cage. The smaller one, Rafiki (which means "friend" in Swahili), looks like a dark, fat plum. Next to him hangs a large tawny-and-golden-furred bat with black stretchy wings named Zuri ("beautiful" in Swahili). Merlin brought them back from one of his trips to Africa, and they have traveled the country with him ever since, in a varnished box with a hot water bottle in the bottom.

Merlin Tuttle with Zuri, a straw-colored flying fox (*Eidolon helvum*).

The two bats are oddly matched companions in that Rafiki belongs to a standoffish species and is very much a loner, whereas Zuri belongs to a deeply affectionate species and is constantly trying to cuddle. Their keepers say that they often see Zuri inching up to Rafiki, who inches away, only to be inched up to again. Once, when Rafiki was sick with an abscessed tooth and a chill, they found Zuri with his wings wrapped completely around the little bat, holding him close to keep him warm and comforted. Today the air conditioning in Merlin's office makes the little bat chilly, and he allows Zuri to sidle up to him and press close, rump to rump. Zuri just lets his wings hang, but Rafiki wraps his wings completely around himself and then latches his thumbs in the back for good measure. I've seen old men stand like this in parks.

Merlin reaches into the cage and pulls Zuri out by unhooking one foot at a time, as if he were lifting two coat hangers out of a closet. Zuri shifts his feet to Merlin's forefinger, and Merlin presses gently with his thumb, just to guard against his flying off and perhaps into a glass window. Zuri is a flying fox, and flying foxes don't echolocate, so they are as vulnerable as birds are to window-bumping. Interestingly enough, both the smallest and the largest of all bats, the bumblebee bats and the flying foxes, share the same Southeast Asian rain forest. Bumblebee bats, weighing a third less than a penny, are also the smallest mammals on earth. Bats often look bigger than they are

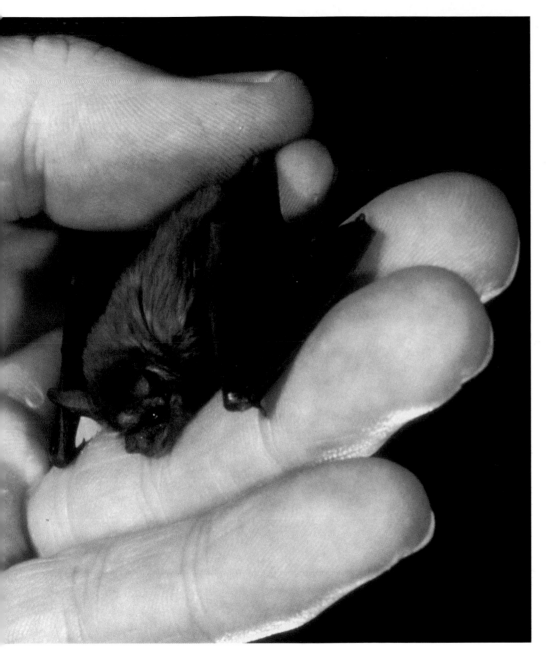

Bumblebee bat (*Craseonycteris thonglongyai*).

Lyle's flying fox (*Pteropus lylei*).

because their wings are so long. But flying foxes can be huge, with wingspans up to six feet wide. Though they don't inhabit the Americas, they're commonplace in a range from West Africa to the Pacific Islands. With familiar foxlike faces and large black eyes, they have small ears and no sonar equipment sticking up from their faces. Fruit-eaters, they've been known to travel as far as sixty miles for food. Orphaned flying foxes that are hand-raised are very affectionate and snuggle up to owners and lick their faces. BCI has members in Australia—"bat mums," as they're called—who have raised injured flying foxes, set them free, and found the bats returning to visit, sometimes to show them their new babies.

Zuri hangs comfortably from Merlin's finger, watching the human pageant.

"Why don't bats faint from hanging upside down?" I ask.

"Why don't we faint from standing right side up?" he retorts. "Why doesn't all the blood rush to our feet? Actually, the bat's better off because he's sure of a good blood supply to the brain."

"Well, do bats do everything upside down?"

"They don't fly upside down," Merlin offers. "Flying foxes even turn right side up to go to the bathroom, so they don't soil themselves."

Hanging down with most of his weight at the bottom, Zuri looks like a half-open umbrella. He turns his head up to look at me with large soulful eyes that hold my gaze. He sneezes. In old wives' tales, bats were thought to tangle in women's hair and drive them insane.

"Want to tangle?" I inquire. We lift him onto my thick curly hair, which he at first slides off of. Finally he hooks his five-toed feet up and hangs down one side of my head as if he were on a motel drape of some sort. Traveling with Merlin, he's had to put his feet up in some odd places, but human hair is clearly not one of his favorites. At last, he creeps around my head a little, and I hear him sneeze gently again from my cologne. Then he wraps around my neck, his tiny claws search my smooth skin for a foothold, and he looks up at me with liquid eyes in which a thousand truths about the rain forest are hidden.

Lifting Zuri onto one finger, I pet his soft neck, and then we put him back in the cage. At once he scuttles over to Rafiki, snuggles rump to rump, and when he's settled, he begins a long, thorough cleaning of his wings, chest, and body, licking methodically like a cat, to get rid of the oils, salt, perfume, and human essence he found on me. It is obvious that he feels dirtied. He washes up slowly, good-naturedly eyeing us, then closes his eyes and begins to doze. After all, it is sleeptime for bats. Nonetheless, when anyone draws near, he opens one eye and peeks out over his arm to see who's there.

African yellow-winged bats roosting in a tree.

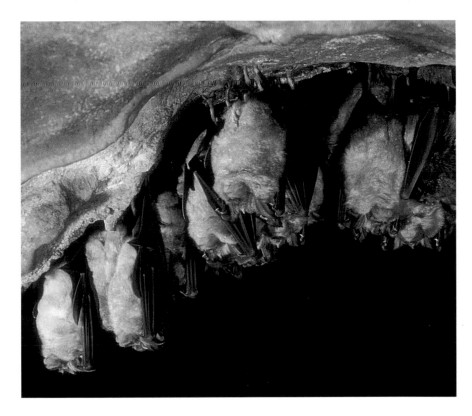

Above left: Gambian epauletted fruit bat and pup.
Above right: Greater horseshoe bats.
Left: Little brown bats.

Bats in Winter

During winter, many species of bats migrate to warmer climates. For example, the Mexican free-tailed bats that live in Bracken Cave travel south to Mexico and Central America, where food is easier to find.

Other bat species hibernate. As they hang in their characteristic upside-down position, their body temperature drops and their breathing and heart rate slow down. In this slowed-down, sleeping state, they use very little energy and can live through the cold winter months, when food is scarce.

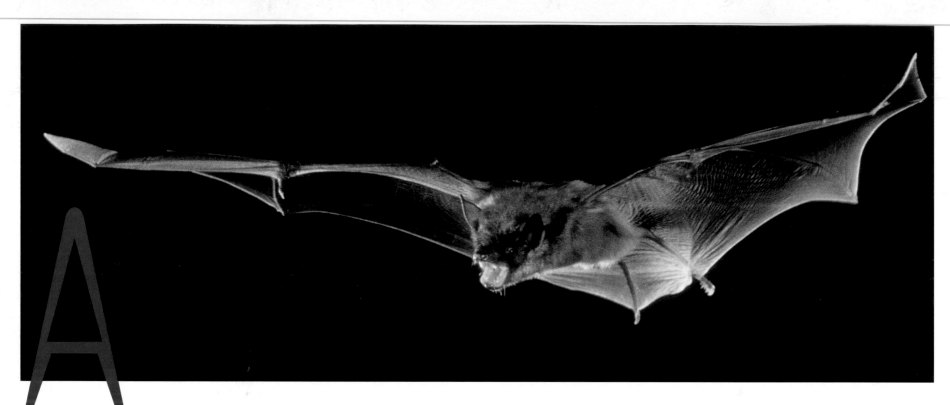

Above: Big brown bat (*Eptesicus fuscus*).
Right: Congress Avenue Bridge at sunset.

At dinnertime, Merlin and I dine on the patio of a downtown hotel beside the Colorado River, a few blocks from the pink granite capitol building and right across from the Congress Avenue Bridge. We have not come for the enchiladas but to watch an "emergence" as dazzling as the one we saw at Bracken Cave. Tucked inside the crevices under the bridge are one and a half million Mexican free-tailed bats. That makes Austin the summer home of the largest urban bat population in the Americas. As the sun ladles thick pastels into the river, two crew boats pull gently side by side. Can they see the bats when they pass under the bridge, I wonder?

Sweethearts have begun to stroll across the bridge hand in hand, waiting for the emergence. Suddenly, smoke billows from underneath the bridge. Not smoke, but a column of bats. Then two columns soar high and fly in parallel, like the long black reins of an invisible sleigh. The bats keep surging out, and soon four columns stretch miles across the sky. A few strays loop and feed near us, passing like shuttles through the weave of the trees. The night is noticeably free of insects, but that's no surprise. These bats will eat more than ten tons of insects tonight alone.

In a medieval story, life is depicted as a beautiful and strange winged creature that appears at a window, flies swiftly through the half-lit banquet hall, and is gone. That seems about right for a vision of creation as beautiful as this one, which now includes the city lights, the four columns of bats undulating across the sky, and the sunset doing a shadow dance over the water. May the world always brim with fascinating animals. May our banquet hall always be filled with bats.

Index

Page numbers in **bold** refer to photographs.

African yellow-winged bat, 14, **14**, **28**

"bat mums," 27
bats:
    diet, 9, 23
    in ecology, 23
    extinct, 23
    handling, 11
    hibernation, 29
    lifespan, 9
    migration, 29
    reproduction, 17
    see also specific species
Bat Conservation International (BCI),
    6, 16, 26, 27
Big Bend National Park, 12, 16–17,
    16
big brown bat, **30**
Bracken Cave, 6, **6**, 25, 29
bumblebee bat, 9, 26, **26**

Chiroptera, 9, 11
common vampire bat, 15, **15**

crested free-tailed bat, 14, **15**
Cuban yellow bat, 23

echolocation, 7, 9, 10, 18, 19, 20, 21
Egyptian fruit bat, 14, **15**, **23**
emergence, 6, **7**, 30
epauletted fruit bat, 12, **12**, **17**, **23**,
    29

flying foxes, 9, 13, **13**, 26–27, **26**, **27**

Grantges, Bert, 16, **18**, 19, 22, **24**, 25
Grantges, Carol, 17
Grantges, Don, 16, 18, 22
greater horseshoe bat, 14, **14**, **29**

Haitian long-tongued bat, 23
hammer-headed fruit bat, **12**, 13

Jamaican long-tongued bat, 23

little brown bat, **2**, 3, 4, **4**, **5**, **29**
long-eared bat, 14–15, **15**
Lyle's flying fox, **27**

Megachiroptera, 9

Mexican free-tailed bat, **1**, 6, **6**, **7**, **8**, 9,
    10, 15, **17**, **21**, 25, **25**, 29
Mexican funnel-eared bat, 13, **13**
Microchiroptera, 9, 19
mini bat-detector, 7, 19, 25
mist net, 18–19, 21, **24**, 25

pallid bat, 22, **22**
Peter's ghost-faced bat, 24, **24**
Puerto Rican long-nosed bat, 23

Rafiki, 26, 28

short-nosed fruit bat, **23**
slit-faced bat, **20**
spectacled flying fox, 13, **13**
spotted bat, 21, **21**
straw-colored flying fox, **26**
sword-nosed bat, 13, **13**

Tuttle, Merlin, 6–7, 9, 10, 11, **11**, 15, 18,
    18, 22, **24**, 25, 26, **26**, 28, 30

Western pipistrelle bat, 19, **19**

Zuri, 26, **26**, 28